General Moshe Dayan

A Photo Salute to Israeli
Hero & Statesman
Moshe Dayan

DR. JOYCE STARR

STARR PUBLISHING

From President Ronald Reagan

"Moshe Dayan provided his nation with military leadership that was the envy of the world. His bold strategies brought him victory on the battlefield and respect from friend and foe alike. His service as a statesman was no less distinguished. He demonstrated those inner qualities of goodwill and integrity that are essential for peace and security.

"Seldom does a foreign general and a statesman receive such admiration from Americans as did Moshe Dayan. His image became to many the symbol of Israeli resolve -- the resolve of a great people to be free and independent, and a resolve shared by the people of the United States."

From Moshe Dayan (1915 - 1977)

"We are a generation that settles the land and without the steel helmet and the canon's maw, we will not be able to plant a tree and build a home ... Let us not avert our eyes lest our arms weaken. This is the fate of our generation. This is our life's choice -- to be prepared and armed, strong and determined, lest the sword be stricken from our fist and our lives cut down."

How Did Moshe Dayan Lose His Eye?

Moshe Dayan joined the Haganah—the pre-state Jewish Defense Forces of Mandatory Palestine—in 1933 at the age of 14, as a member of the Jewish Auxiliary Police. He served in the Special Night Squads under British General Orde Wingate during the Arab riots in Palestine (1936-39). He lost an eye in 1941 during the British Empire forces raid on Vichy forces in Lebanon during World War II.

Dayan was looking through his binoculars when a sniper's bullet hit him in the eye. After recuperating in the hospital for several months, he returned to active duty, serving as Commander of the Jerusalem front in the 1948 Arab–Israeli War, IDF Chief of Staff during the 1956 Suez Crisis, and Defense Minister during both the Six-Day War of 1967 and the Yom Kippur War of 1973. Three "Dayans" were elected to the Israeli Knesset: Moshe Dayan, his father Shmuel Dayan and his daughter Yael Dayan.

From the Author

I am honored to say that I'm related to Moshe Dayan. I learned this after he passed away. While I did not have the privilege of meeting him, our paths crossed in both Washington and Israel—separated by less than 30 feet on several occasions. This book is a testimony to Jewish heritage and another step forward in my lifelong embrace of Israel.

Sgan Aluf (Lt. Col.) Moshe Dayan.
July 5, 1948 / Hans Pin

Sgan Aluf (Lt. Col.) Moshe Dayan with
P.M. David Ben-Gurion. July 4, 1948 / David Eldan

Sgan Aluf (Lt. Col.) Moshe Dayan
at Settlement Day Celebrations,
Kibbutz Maale Hahamisha.
October 23, 1948 / Photographer Unknown

Rav Aluf (Lt. Gen.) Moshe Dayan, Member of the
Israel-Rhodes Mission, Returns to Tel Aviv.
April 4, 1949 / David El Dan

Mixed Armistice Commission of 1949.
During the Waiting Period, Rav aluf (Lt. Gen.)
Moshe Dayan Talks with His Secretary,
Major Basil Herman (Center) Near Tulkarem,
a Palestinian City in the West Bank.
May 7, 1949 / Photographer Unknown

Aluf Mishneh (Col.) Moshe Dayan with
Captain Nachid of the Egyptian Delegation to the
Egyptian-Israel Mixed Armistice Commissions.
March 22, 1950 / Fritz Cohen

Heikh Suleiman El Hezail (Center) Entertains
Chief of Staff Yigal Yadin (Left), Aluf Moshe Dayan (Right)
& Dayan's First Wife, Mrs. Ruth Dayan (Right),
at His Bedouin Village in the Negev Desert.
May 2, 1950 / Fritz Cohen

Overcome by Emotion, Prime Minister David
Ben-Gurion (Center) Hugs the Out Going Chief
of Staff Mordechai Makleff (Right).
Rav Aluf Moshe Dayan (Left) Looks on.
Beit Hanassi, Jerusalem.
December 6, 1953 / David Eldan

Newly Appointed Chief of Staff Rav Aluf
(Lt. Gen.) Moshe Dayan (Right),
Prime Minister David Ben-Gurion (Center)
& Outgoing Chief of Staff Rav Aluf
(Lt. Gen.) Mordechai Makeleff, LP (Left).
Beit Hanassi, Jerusalem.
December 12, 1953 / David Eldan

Chief of Staff, Moshe Dayan During a Relaxed
Moment While Visiting with New IDF Recruits
at the Bahad 4 Military Base, Ashkelon.
February 10, 1954 / Photographer Unknown

Chief of Staff Moshe Dayan.
July 5, 1954 / David Eldan

RavAluf (Lt. Gen.) Moshe Dayan with
His Son Ehud (Udi) & His Parents at Lydda Airport,
Prior to Boarding a Plane for the U.S.
July 11, 1954 / Hans Pins

Minister of Defense David Ben-Gurion,
Chief of Staff Moshe Dayan (Left) &
Dir. General of Defense, Minister Shimon Peres
at the Hakirya (IDF headquarters) in Tel Aviv.
February 2, 1955 / Hans Pin

Having Lunch with His Wife Ruth in Tel Aviv.
October 4, 1955 / Photographer Unknown

Prime Minister David Ben-Gurion
& Chief of Staff Moshe Dayan
Inspect the Honor Guard at the
Prime Minister's Office in Tel Aviv.
February 20, 1955 / Hans Pinn

Chief of Staff Moshe Dayan Digging
Trenches at Border Settlement Mivtachim
March 8, 1956 / Fritz Cohen

Chief of Staff Moshe Dayan Visiting
Troops at Sharem El Sheik in the Sinai.
November 11, 1956 / Photographer Unknown

Chief of Staff Moshe Dayan & Defense Ministry
Director Shimon Peres at the Beit Dagon
Arms Exhibition, Tel Aviv.
April 29, 1957 / Moshe Pridan

IDF Chief of Staff Moshe Dayan.
May 1, 1957 / Moshe Pridan

Chief of Staff Moshe Dayan Inspects Newly
Graduated Officers at the Israel Defense Forces
Honor Guard Ceremony in Tel Aviv.
August 10, 1957 / Photographer Unknown

Prime Minister David Ben-Gurion
Pins the Haganah Medal on Chief of Staff
Moshe Dayan in Jerusalem.
June 9, 1958 / Moshe Pridan

Six Day War.
Defense Min. Moshe Dayan (Center),
Commander Yitzhak Rabin (Right)
& Commander Uzi Narkis (Left) enter the
Lions Gate into the Old City of Jerusalem.
June 6, 1967 / Ilan Bruner

Six Day War.
Defense Minister Moshe Dayan
& Jerusalem Commander Uzi Narkis
under the Street Sign Pointing to
the Western Wall in Jerusalem.
June 7, 1967 / Ilan Bluner

AL-BURÁQ
(WAILING WALL) RD.

Defense Minister Moshe Dayan
Standing Under the "Welcome to Bethlehem"
Banner at the Entrance to the Town.
June 8, 1967 / Moshe Milner

With His Daughter Yael in the Sinai.
Assaf Kutan / June 14, 1967

Defense Minister Moshe Dayan (Left) Reading
the Order for the Day to Senior Commanders of the
Israel Defense Forces Near the Western Wall
in the Old City of Jerusalem.
June 12, 1967 / Ilan Bruner

Former U.S. Vice President Richard Nixon with
Minister of Defense Moshe Dayan
at the Ministry of Defense in Tel Aviv.
June 22, 1967 / Ilan Bruner

Prime Minister Golda Meir with Defense Minister
Moshe Dayan & Chief of Staff Bar Lev at the
Beit Hanassi (Prime Minister's Office) in Jerusalem.
April 23, 1969 / Moshe Milner

Defense Minister Dayan (Center), Flanked by
Chief of Staff Haim Bar Lev (2nd. Left) & Air Force
Commander Mordechai Hold (2nd Right), Arriving
at the Air Force Day Ceremony in Tel Aviv.
July 17, 1969 / Moshe Milner

Defense Minister Moshe Dayan, 1969.
Photographer Unknown.

David Ben-Gurion & Defense Minister Moshe Dayan
at the Induction Ceremony for Ashkenazi
Chief Rabbi Shlomo Goren in Tel Aviv.
June 15, 1971 / Fritz Cohen

Defense Minister Moshe Dayan (Right),
Chief of Staff Haim Bar Lev (Far Right) &
Senior Staff Officers at an Observation Post
During Maneuvers of the Northern Command.
June 17, 1971 / Moshe Milner

Defense Minister Moshe Dayan Looking Out
From the Terrace of the Library Building
in the College of the Negev at SdeBoker.
October 6, 1971 / Fritz Cohen

Defense Minister Moshe Dayan Joining the Crowds
During the "Mimouna" Celebration in Jerusalem.
Mimouna is a Traditional Dinner for Jews of
Maghrebi Heritage in Morocco, Israel, France, Canada,
& Worldwide. Held the Day after Passover,
it Marks the Return to Eating Hametz (Leavened
Bread)—Forbidden During Passover.
April 24, 1973 / Herman Chanania

The Yom Kippur War Begins.
Defense Minister Moshe Dayan During His Press
Conference After the Outbreak of Hostilities
Along the Syrian & Egyptian Frontiers.
The War was Initiated by Syria & Egypt on the
Jewish Holy Day of Yom Kippur.
October 6, 1973 / Herman Chanania

Yom Kippur War.
A General Staff Meeting in the "War Room".
Defense Minister Dayan (Center) with
Aluf (Gen.) Rehavam Zeevy &
Aluf (Gen.) Shumel Gonen.
October 8, 1973 / Shlomo Arad

Yom Kippur War.
Chief of Staff Haim Bar-Lev (Center Left)
& Defense Min. Moshe Dayan (Center) Consult
with Maj. Gen. Ariel Sharon (Bandage) in the Sinai.
October 17, 1973 / Yossi Greenberg

Yom Kippur War.
Before Crossing the Suez Canal on October 17th, 1973, the Divisional HQ Posed for a Photograph. General Moshe Dayan (Center) is Surrounded by Gen. Ariel Sharon (Left with Bandage), Commanding Officer of "The Crossing Division - 143," Senior Div. Staff Officers & Troops. Photo Inscription: "To Zalman, In Deep Friendship, Moshe Dayan." Zalman Enav was Special Assistant to Ariel Sharon During the War and a Member of the Israeli Delegations to Military Talks with Egypt, 1973-74, 1975, 1978-79 (Camp David Peace Process)
with the Rank of Major.
Photo Courtesy of Zalman Enav

Yom Kippur War. Defense Minister Moshe Dayan Speaks with
an IDF Soldier at an IDF Outpost in the Sinai Desert.
October 17, 1973 / Yossi Greenberg

Yom Kippur War.
Defense Minister Moshe Dayan &
Aluf (Gen.) Avraham Adan at an
IDF Outpost the Suez Canal.
October 29, 1973 / Yehuda Tzion

Yom Kippur War.
Defense Minister Moshe Dayan (Left) & Aluf (Gen.)
Yitzhak Hoffi, Head of the Northern Command (Right),
Sharing a Drink with Soldiers on the Golan Heights.
November 11, 1973 / Ron Frenkel

Tel Aviv Mayor Shlomo Lahat with Yael & Assi,
Children of Member of Knesset Moshe Dayan
in the Shahaf Cinema in Tel Aviv.
Mrs. Rachel Dayan sits at the left.
Ya'acov Sa'ar. March 17, 1977

Knesset Member Menachem Begin (Left),
Knesset Member Moshe Dayan (Center),
South African Prime Minister John Vorster (Right)
& Prime Minister Yitzhak Rabin (Far Right)
During a Reception at the Hilton Hotel in Jerusalem.
April 4, 1977 / Ya'acov Sa'ar

U.S. Secretary of State Cyrus Vance (Left) &
Foreign Minister Moshe Dayan (Center) are Led
to the Prime Minister's Office in Jerusalem
by Prime Minister Menachem Begin (Right).
August 9, 1977 / Moshe Milner

Egyptian President Anwar Sadat (Right)
& Foreign Minister Moshe Dayan (Left)
at the King David Hotel in Jerusalem.
November 19, 1977 / Ya'Acov Sa'Ar

Foreign Min. Moshe Dayan &
Prime Minister Menachem Begin
on a flight from Lod to Ismalia, Egypt for
Camp David Peace Process Negotiations.
December 25, 1977 / Ya'acov Sa'ar

Foreign Minister Moshe Dayan (Left),
President Jimmy Carter (Center) &
Egyptian Defense Minister Kamal Ali (Right)
at a White House Peace Negotiations
Press Conference in Washington, D.C.
October 26, 1978 / Robert A. Cumins

7 BONUS PHOTOS

War of Independence

1947 - 1949

52

The Haganah Ship "Exodus 1947".
Even the Few Belongings of Children
Were Searched for Weapons.
June 1, 1947 / Photographer Unknown

The Haganah Ship "Exodus 1947".
A Young Couple Walks to the Deportation Facility.

"British soldiers removed Jews from the Exodus in the port of Haifa on the 18th of July 1947. After two days, the illegal immigrants were deported to France on three boats, and from there to Germany, where most were set down on the beach. Most of the deportees stayed in camps in Germany for over a year, and reached Israel only after the establishment of the State." - yadvashem.org/holocaust/this-month/july/1947.html

Jerusalemites Celebrate the United Nations
Decision on the Partition of Palestine on Top of
an Armored Israeli Police Car.
November 30, 1947 / Hans Pinn

Prime Minister David Ben-Gurion Signs the
Scroll of the Declaration of Independence
with Rabbi Yehuda Leib Hacohen Looking on
During the Ceremony in the Tel Aviv Museum.
May 14, 1948 / Hans Pinn

The War of Independence.
Haganah Members Hoist the Flag of the
State of Israel on Top of the Jaffa Lighthouse
After the Town's Surrender.
May 15, 1948 / Hanns Pinn

The Torah—The First Five Books of Moses—Penetrated
by Shells During an Arab Attack.
July 1, 1948 / Photographer Unknown

All the books of Torah are divine works, yet the First Five
Books hold a unique place as the work of Moses. "The veracity
of the Moses' prophecy is based on a national experience—an
event at Mount Sinai in which the entire nation witnessed G-d
communicating with him."

chabad.org/library/article_cdo/aid/1426382/jewish/Torah.htm

תורה
נביאים וכתובים

Independence Day Parade, 1949.
Tel Avivians Crowd Windows, Tree Tops
& Roofs Waiting for the Parade.
May 4, 1949 / Hans Pinn

About the Author

Dr. Joyce Starr has authored 31 books on compelling topics—including her ten-book Israel Series—and produced a dozen travel journals featuring historic Israel and Holyland covers. Visit DrJoyceStarr.com and her Amazon Israel Series (linked to this book) to learn more. She curated/published both *General Moshe Dayan: A Photo Salute to Israeli Hero & Statesman Moshe Dayan* and *Golda: A Photo Journey with Golda Meir* to preserve photos that might be lost to current and future generations.